Máquinas maravillosas/Mighty Machines

Barredoras de nieve/Snowplows

por/by Terri DeGezelle

Traducción/Translation: Dr. Martín Luis Guzmán Ferrer
Editor Consultor/Consulting Editor: Dra. Gail Saunders-Smith

Consultor/Consultant: Tammy Higham, CAE
Snow and Ice Management Association
Erie, Pennsylvania

Capstone press®

Mankato, Minnesota

Pebble Plus is published by Capstone Press,
151 Good Counsel Drive, P.O. Box 669, Mankato, Minnesota 56002.
www.capstonepress.com

1 2 3 4 5 6 11 10 09 08 07 06

Library of Congress Cataloging-in-Publication Data
DeGezelle, Terri, 1955–
    [Snowplows. Spanish & English]
    Barredoras de nieve = Snowplows/de Terri DeGezelle.
    p. cm.—(Pebble plus. Máquinas maravillosas = Pebble plus. Mighty machines)
    Includes index.
    ISBN-13: 978-0-7368-6674-3 (hardcover)
    ISBN-10: 0-7368-6674-4 (hardcover)
    1. Snowplows—Juvenile literature. 2. Snow removal—Juvenile literature. I. Title: Snowplows. II. Title. III.
Pebble plus. Máquinas maravillosas. IV. Pebble plus. Mighty machines.
TD868.D4418 2007
629.225—dc22   2005037463

Summary: Simple text and photographs present snowplows and the work they do—in both English
    and Spanish.

Editorial Credits
Martha E. H. Rustad, editor; Katy Kudela, bilingual editor; Eida del Risco, Spanish copy editor; Molly Nei,
    set designer; Ted Williams, book designer; Wanda Winch, photo researcher; Scott Thoms, photo editor

Photo Credits
Capstone Press/Karon Dubke, cover; Corbis/Reuters, 7; Digital Vision Ltd., 1; The Image Works/Chet
Gordon, 13; The Image Works/David M. Jennings, 17; The Image Works/Syracuse Newspapers/John Berry, 11;
iStockphoto Inc./Benoit Beauregar, 21; Peter Arnold, Inc./Craig Newbauer, 19; Photri-MicroStock/M. Boroff, 15;
SuperStock/age fotostock, 9; Wolfgang Kaehler, 5

The author thanks Jerry O'Meara, Heavy Equipment Operator, City of Mankato, Minnesota, for his assistance
with this book. Pebble Plus thanks Jerry Strobel, Street Maintenance, City of Glencoe, Minnesota, for his
assistance with this book. Pebble Plus also thanks the Hennepin County Highway Department for assistance
with photo shoots.

Note to Parents and Teachers

The Máquinas maravillosas/Mighty Machines set supports national standards related
to science, technology, and society. This book describes snowplows in both English and
Spanish. The images support early readers in understanding the text. The repetition of
words and phrases helps early readers learn new words. This book also introduces early
readers to subject-specific vocabulary words, which are defined in the Glossary section.
Early readers may need assistance to read some words and to use the Table of Contents,
Glossary, Internet Sites, and Index sections of the book.

Table of Contents

Tabla de contenidos

A Snowplow's Job

Snowplows clear snow away
after snowstorms.
Snowplows make snowy roads
safe for travel.

Cómo trabaja una barredora de nieve

Las barredoras de nieve quitan la nieve
después de las nevadas. Las barredoras
de nieve hacen que sea más seguro
viajar por las carreteras nevadas.

4

Snowplows push snow off airport runways.

They clear parking lots and driveways.

Las barredoras de nieve quitan la nieve
de las pistas de los aeropuertos. También
la quitan de los estacionamientos y
las entradas de las casas.

Parts of Snowplows

Snowplow blades scrape up snow.
They push the snow
to the side of the road.

Las partes de las barredoras de nieve

Las hojas de las barredoras de nieve
raspan la nieve. También empujan
la nieve a los lados de la carretera.

Snowplow drivers sit in the cab.

They use levers to move the blade.

El conductor de la barredora

de nieve se sienta en la cabina.

Él usa palancas para mover las hojas.

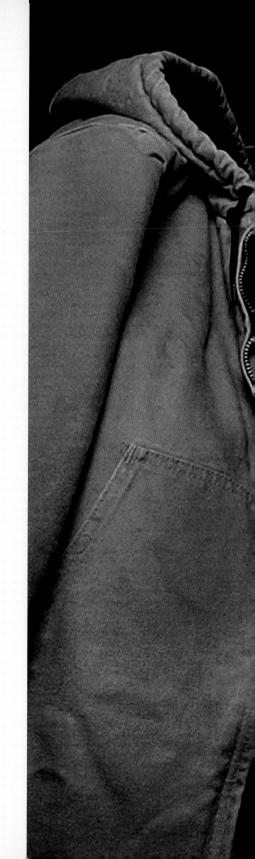

Snowplows have flashing lights.
The lights warn people
to be careful around snowplows.

Las barredoras de nieve tienen luces
intermitentes. Las luces advierten a
las personas que sean cuidadosas
cuando estén cerca de una barredora.

Big snowblowers work on highways.
They have turning blades
that blow snow off roads.

Los grandes ventiladores de nieve
trabajan en las carreteras. Estos
tienen unas hojas que giran y
quitan la nieve de las carreteras.

blade/hoja

15

What Snowplows Do

Groups of snowplows
work together to clear
big roads quickly.

Qué hacen las barredoras de nieve

Las barredoras de nieve trabajan
en grupos para despejar rápidamente
las grandes carreteras.

Snowplows clear the way for spreader trucks.
Spreader trucks drop sand or salt on roads.
Sand and salt make icy roads safer for travel.

Las barredoras de nieve limpian las carreteras
para que los camiones esparcidores puedan entrar.
Los camiones esparcidores echan arena y sal en
las carreteras. La arena y la sal permiten viajar
con más seguridad por las carreteras heladas.

Mighty Snowplows

Snowplows make winter roads
safe for cars and trucks.
Snowplows are mighty machines.

Maravillosas barredoras de nieve

Las barredoras de nieve hacen que en
invierno las carreteras sean seguras para
los autos y camiones. Las barredoras
de nieve son unas máquinas maravillosas.

Glossary

blade—a sharp piece of metal on a snowplow that pushes snow; blades on snowblowers turn to blow snow off roads.

cab—an enclosed area of a truck or other vehicle where the driver sits

flashing—turning on and off

lever—a bar or handle used to control a machine

runway—a long, flat strip of ground where airplanes take off and land

warn—to tell people about danger

Glosario

advertir—decirles a las personas que hay peligro

la cabina—lugar cerrado donde el conductor se sienta, ya sea en un camión o en otro vehículo

la hoja—pieza filosa de metal de la barredora de nieve que quita la nieve; las hojas de la barredora de nieve giran y amontonan la nieve a los lados de las carreteras.

intermitente—que se prende y se apaga

la palanca—barra o manija para operar una máquina

la pista—una franja de terreno plana y alargada donde los aviones aterrizan y despegan

Internet Sites

FactHound offers a safe, fun way to find Internet sites related to this book. All of the sites on FactHound have been researched by our staff.

Here's how:

1. Visit *www.facthound.com*

2. Choose your grade level.

3. Type in this book ID **0736866744** for age-appropriate sites. You may also browse subjects by clicking on letters, or by clicking on pictures and words.

4. Click on the **Fetch It** button.

FactHound will fetch the best sites for you!

Index

Sitios de Internet

FactHound proporciona una manera divertida y segura de encontrar sitios de Internet relacionados con este libro. Nuestro personal ha investigado todos los sitios de FactHound. Es posible que los sitios no estén en español.

Se hace así:

1. Visita *www.facthound.com*

2. Elige tu grado escolar.

3. Introduce este código especial **0736866744** para ver sitios apropiados según tu edad, o usa una palabra relacionada con este libro para hacer una búsqueda general.

4. Haz clic en el botón **Fetch It**.

¡FactHound buscará los mejores sitios para ti!

Índice